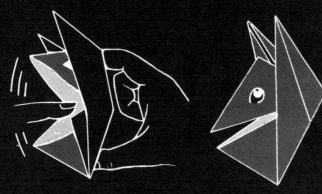

FOLDING
PAPER
PUPPETS

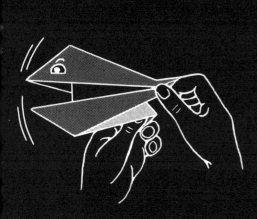

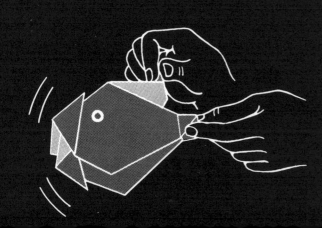
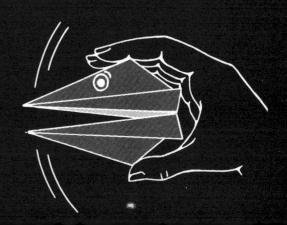

FOLDING

Distributed by J. B. Lippincott Company, Philadelphia 5

BY *Shari Lewis*

AND *Lillian Oppenheimer*

PAPER
PUPPETS

𝕾𝕯 STEIN AND DAY / *Publishers* / New York

Drawings by Dorothy Anderson

Photographs by Ray Buckner

Designed by David Miller

Printed in the United States of America.

DEDICATION

To the joyous memory of Harry Oppenheimer

CONTENTS

ABOUT FOLDING PAPER PUPPETS

by SHARI LEWIS

On a recent airplane flight from Los Angeles to New York, my attention was drawn to a five-year-old girl, seated across the aisle. She was weeping inconsolably, while her ten-year-old brother sat beside her, fiddling contentedly with a folded paper glider. Since she was holding a piece of paper, I called the child over and tried to amuse her by folding a flapping bird out of her own piece of paper.

To my utter astonishment, she now wept harder and louder than ever. I led her back to her mother and asked why she was crying so. Her mother told me that during their two week visit to grandmother's in Hollywood, the little girl had received two autographs, one from Shirley Temple and the other from Roy Rogers. She was crying because her brother had made a glider out of one, and I had just folded a bird out of the other!

And that, believe it or not, is the only unhappy experience I've ever had with Origami. In fact, my interest in folding paper puppets, figures, and toys has brought me much pleasure and many friends.

Here are some of the ways in which I've enjoyed using classic techniques of Origami.

AS A CRAFT PROJECT

Origami offers the hobbyist many rewards — the stimulation of working with beautiful basic materials (papers of various colors, textures, and designs), the relaxation of utter involvement in the activity of folding, the challenge of attempting a new design, the satisfaction of the lovely finished product, and the exciting sense of having participated in an art form of another culture.

Paperfolding is also an excellent aid to the development of manual dexterity. There is something tremendously reassuring to amateur craftsmen in the symmetry of Origami, for a given fold at one end of the paper is generally repeated at the other end. Very heartening as well is the knowledge that, once mastered, the standard folds are used again and again in the creation of many paper figures. Another important factor in the cultivation of self-confidence is the satisfaction of seeing a project through to completion, and the speed with which an attractive Origami figure can be made is very rewarding indeed. Fortunately too, the materials are inexpensive, for this minimizes the importance of a mistake and encourages experimentation.

AS A CREATIVE ART FORM

The development of creativity is dependent in part upon the artistic potential of the individual. No amount of training will guarantee that a pupil will be able to paint, choreograph, compose, or design well, or produce an original work of art. But a degree of artistic originality, and an appreciation of beauty can and should be encouraged, and Origami is an admirable tool toward this end, for there is a universal pleasure to be derived from the handling of the lushly colored papers and from the selection of just the right texture or design to suit the finished object. Moreover, the completed paperfold is a reduction of a recognizable object to its most beautiful organic lines. These lovely semi-abstract figures can be utilized to good advantage in collages, posters, and mobiles. The Flapping Bird (page 64), lends itself to the mobile most exquisitely. Also the Talking Fish (page 42), Whale (page 24), and Crow (page 18).

AS A DECORATIVE ART FORM

Creative self-expression often requires an incentive; the need for decorative holiday and party items can provide a concrete stimulation to a latent or timid artistic inclination. Moreover, paperfold figures, fashioned in fabulous colors and unusual sizes, are less expensive and generally more beautiful than similar items which are commercially available. Here are some ways in which figures included in this book can be employed for decorative purposes:

1. *Christmas Tree Decorations*
   Flapping Birds (page 64) look extremely graceful hanging from branches of a Christmas tree, as do the Crow (page 18), Pecking Chicken (page 21), Whale (page 24), and Talking Fish (page 42).

2. *Greeting Cards*
   Holiday greetings can be written on the wings, necks, and bodies of the Crow (page 18), Whale (page 24), Talking Fish (page 42), and Flapping Bird (page 64). The Rabbit (page 28), presents interesting possibilities as an Easter greeting. All of these figures are flat, and can be slipped

into an envelope with ease. They can also be pasted to the face of a plain or painted card, with the salutation written on the inside or on the reverse side of the card.

3. *Party Decorations*

Place cards can be made with the Crow (page 18), Pecking Chicken (page 21), Whale (page 24), Flapping Bird (page 64), and Simple Sue (page 71). For party favors, try the Bloodhound (page 27), Talking Fish (page 42), and Snap Dragon (page 52).

A colorful centerpiece for a party table can be created by setting a large black Crow (page 18) in the center of a big bowl of popcorn or by nesting an enormous Flapping Bird (page 64) on a dish of gumdrops, round fruits or jelly beans.

Masks can be made by folding the Pig (page 56) out of a piece of paper at least 15 inches square and attaching string or elastic under the Pig's ears and cutting peepholes. To make the mask use colored shelf paper or gift wrapping paper.

AS A THERAPEUTIC ACTIVITY

Many vocational therapists say that the novelty of Origami often makes it easier to communicate with individuals whose spirits have been dulled by mental or physical illness. My own experience in teaching Origami to bed-ridden youngsters has shown me that this inactive activity can keep restless children happily occupied for hours. Incidentally, the fact that only paper is required (no scissors, no paste) makes paperfolding a safe as well as sanitary sick-bed pastime.

AS A FORM OF ENTERTAINMENT

If you're a pianist, you can't perform without a piano. A dancer must have floor space and accompaniment, and even a magician appreciates the presence of a pet rabbit. But a paper folder requires only a sheet of paper in order to delight an audience.

I've folded paper puppets for my own amusement, and for the entertainment of others on TV, at parties, in classrooms and hospital wards, and at dinner tables. In Japan, my husband and I even spent two amusing hours on a train doing Origami with a dozen Japanese high school students who had befriended us.

Parents and grandparents often find that their ability to make a paper puppet or toy causes youngsters to view them with a new interest. And teachers and group leaders use animated Origami figures to illustrate simple dramatic projects. Story telling can be made more theatrically exciting by folding paper puppets in the forms of the leading characters and manipulating them as the tale is told. Stories based upon animal characters are most appropriate. I recommend:

Aesop's Fables (including "The Fox and the Sour Grapes," "The Crow and the Pitcher," "The Fox and the Cat," etc.)
La Fontaine Tales (such as "The Fox and the Crow," and "The Stork and the Fox")
The Brer Rabbit Stories (particularly those involving the Fox and the Rabbit)
Tales from the Arabian Nights ("The Talking Fish," etc.)
Bible Stories (including "Noah" and "Jonah and the Whale")
Old Fairy Tales ("Puss in Boots," "Three Little Pigs," "Wild Swans," "Ugly Duckling," etc.)

And now that I've presented these modern adaptations of the ancient art of Origami, I would like to say what my friend Lillian Oppenheimer always says to someone new to the hobby. If you ask her to describe its virtues and values, she will hand you a pretty square of paper and say, "Fold along with me, and you'll see!"

BASIC RULES

OF ORIGAMI

1. Choose a flat, hard surface as your place of work.

2. Be sure to make your folds straight.

3. Make your creases sharp by pressing along them with your thumbnail.

4. If possible choose a paper with a color, texture, and design that will add beauty and interest to your model.

5. Do experiment with different kinds of paper. Try typing paper, onion skin paper, gift wrapping and shelf paper, magazine pages or covers, colored comics, and even stiff fabrics like buckram for a variety of effects.

Kite Fold Base

The kite fold base, and all of the puppets made from it, start with a square piece of paper.

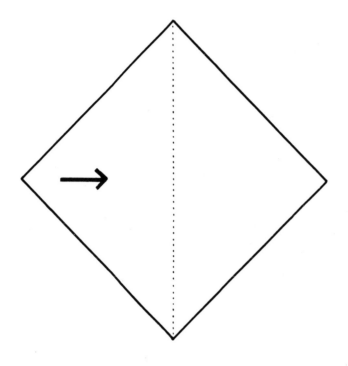

1

Bring one side corner to meet the other, and crease sharply on the diagonal.

2

Open the paper to the starting position.

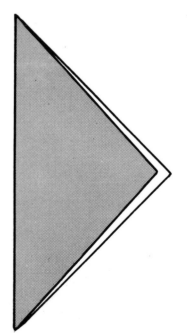

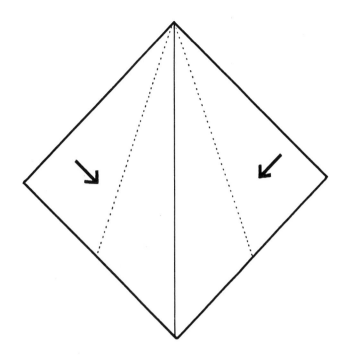

3

Fold the right and left top edges of your paper to the center crease.

4

This is the kite fold base.

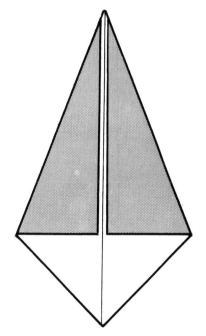

HUNGRY CROW

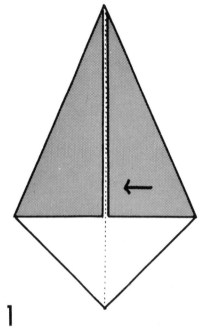

1

Fold the kite fold base in half along the center crease.

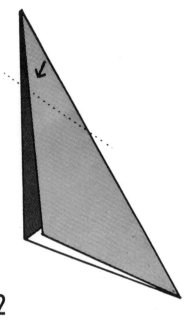

2

At an angle one-third of the way down the center fold, crease the top point back and forth, and then straighten the point. You have created a slanting crease.

4

Your Crow will balance on his nose and the two center points. If you tap his tail gently, he will peck at tiny crumpled balls of paper.

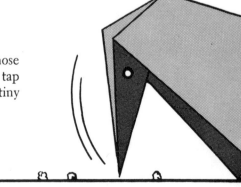

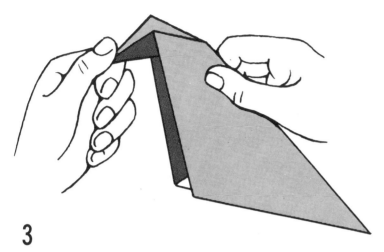

3

With your right hand, pinch the center fold directly below this slanting crease. Curve the pointer (index) finger of your left hand and place it in the pocket at the top, opening the center crease. Put your left thumb on top of the center crease, grasping the point between these two fingers and pull down until the center crease reverses itself and forms a valley between your two hands. With your left hand, sharpen all these new creases.

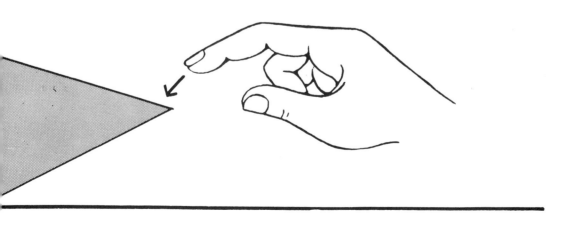

A photograph of the finished puppet is on the next page ▷

HUNGRY CROW

PECKING CHICKEN

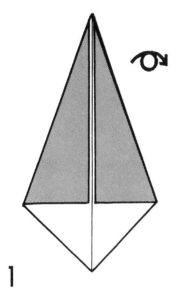

1

Turn the kite fold base over.

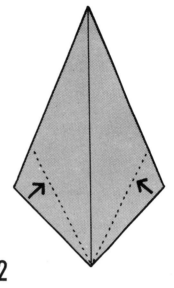

2

Fold the right and left bottom edges of paper to the center crease.

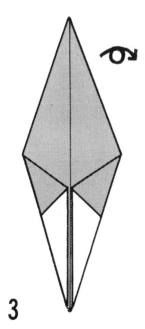

3

Turn the paper over.

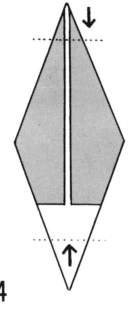

4

Fold the top point down and the bottom point up.

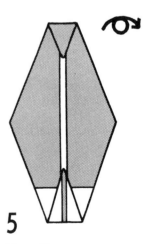

5

Turn the paper over.

PECKING CHICKEN **Continued** ▷

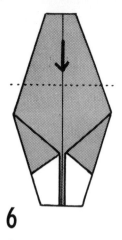

6

Fold the top down.

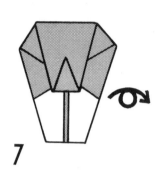

7

Turn the paper over.

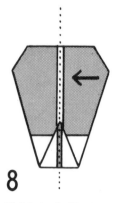

8

Fold in half along the center crease.

9

The neck and head are lying along the side. First, pull the head out and sharpen your creases so that the head remains in this position.

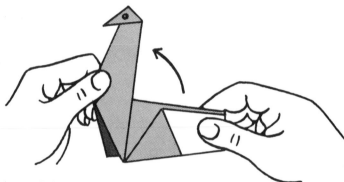

10 Pinching the head, pull until the neck is perpendicular to the body. Sharpen the creases at the breast and turn your Chicken to an upright position.

11 Insert your thumb and pointer finger into the two side pockets. Your middle finger, resting outside the pocket containing your pointer finger, will help control the movement of the chicken. Just separate your thumb and pointer finger and bring them together again, and your Chicken will nod and peck. If you moisten your finger tips slightly, you'll have better control of the Chicken's movement.

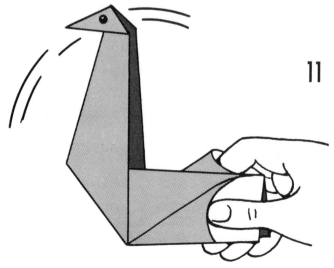

Original paper puppet created by Joyce Rockmore

PECKING CHICKEN

WHALE

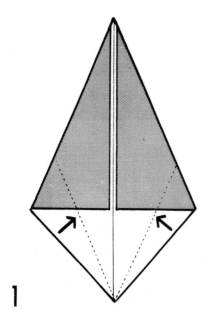

1

Fold the right and left bottom edges of the kite fold base to the center crease.

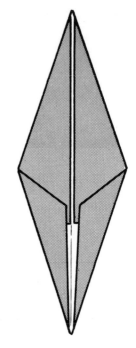

2

Now open the entire piece of paper.

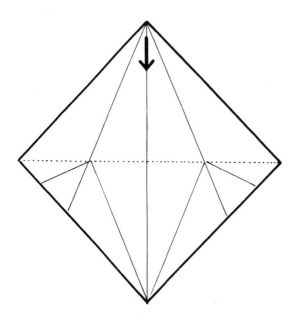

3

Bring the top point down to meet the bottom point, crease along the diagonal, and then reopen the paper.

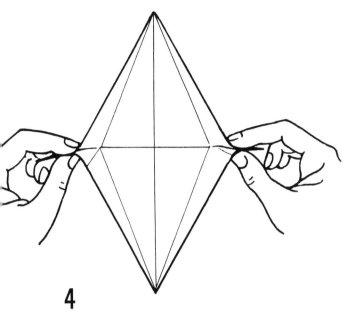

4

Place your thumb and pointer finger under the paper at each side corner, pinching the center fold closed at these points.

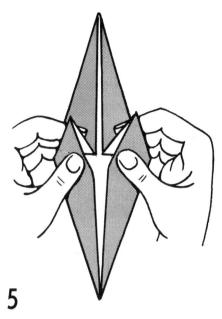

5

Brings your hands (and these side points) together in front of the paper and sharpen your creases so that the paper remains in this position. You now have two small standing flaps in the center.

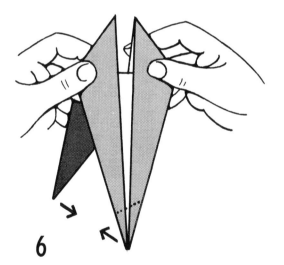

6

Hold these small center flaps between your thumbs and pointer fingers. Place your middle fingers under the paper at each side along the small center crease. Now fold the large upper point back (away from you) until it meets the large bottom point. Crease sharply.

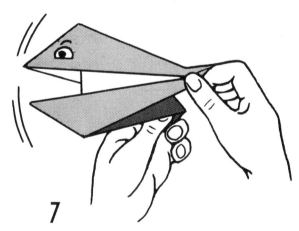

7

Turn your Whale to a swimming position and fold the top flap of his tail up at an angle. Turn your whale over and fold the other tail flap so that it points in the opposite direction.

Grasp one tail flap in each hand and, as you move your hands apart and together, your Whale will talk.

A photograph of the finished puppet is on the next page ▷

WHALE

BLOODHOUND

Start with the kite fold base, and then do steps 1 through 6 of the whale (page 24)

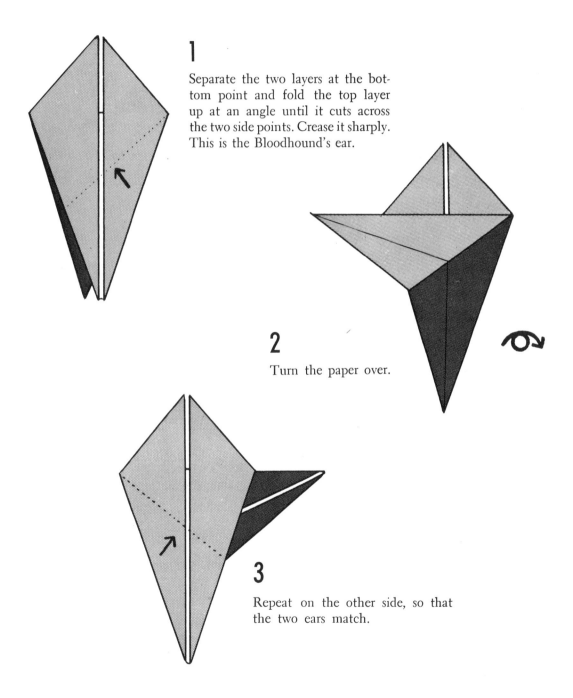

1

Separate the two layers at the bottom point and fold the top layer up at an angle until it cuts across the two side points. Crease it sharply. This is the Bloodhound's ear.

2

Turn the paper over.

3

Repeat on the other side, so that the two ears match.

BLOODHOUND *Continued* ▷

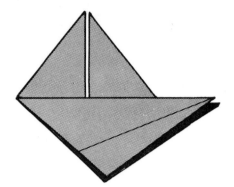

4

Turn your Bloodhound so that his ears hang down.

5

Hold each ear — not at the bottom, but at the back point. Move your hands apart and together and the Bloodhound will bark (very quietly of course!).

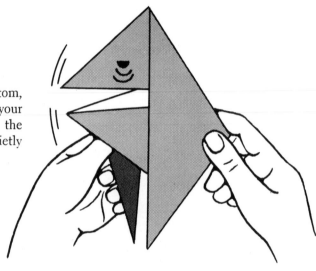

6

Turn the completed paperfold so that the ears point up. Hold them in the same way as the Bloodhound and you have a Talkative Rabbit.

Double Diagonal Base

The double diagonal base, and all of the puppets made from it, start with a square piece of paper.

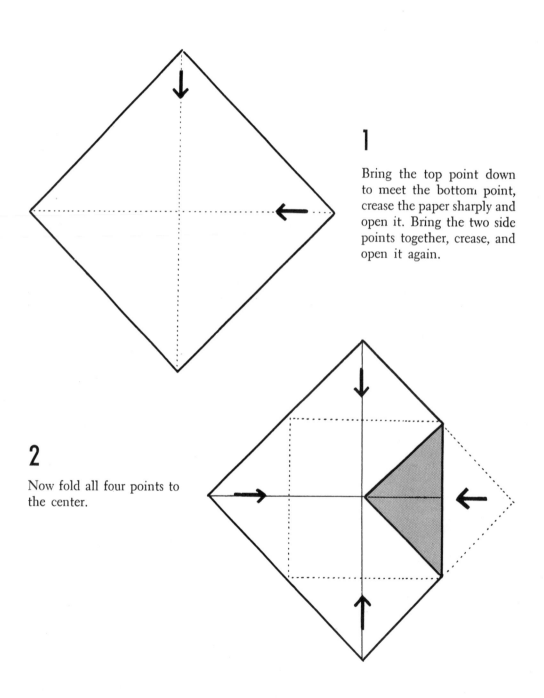

1

Bring the top point down to meet the bottom point, crease the paper sharply and open it. Bring the two side points together, crease, and open it again.

2

Now fold all four points to the center.

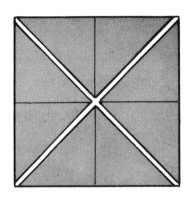

3

Turn the folded paper over.

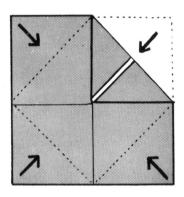

4

Fold each of these new points to the center.

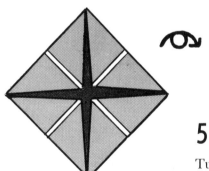

5

Turn the paper over again.

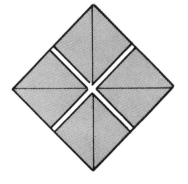

6

This is the double diagonal base.

EATING BIRD

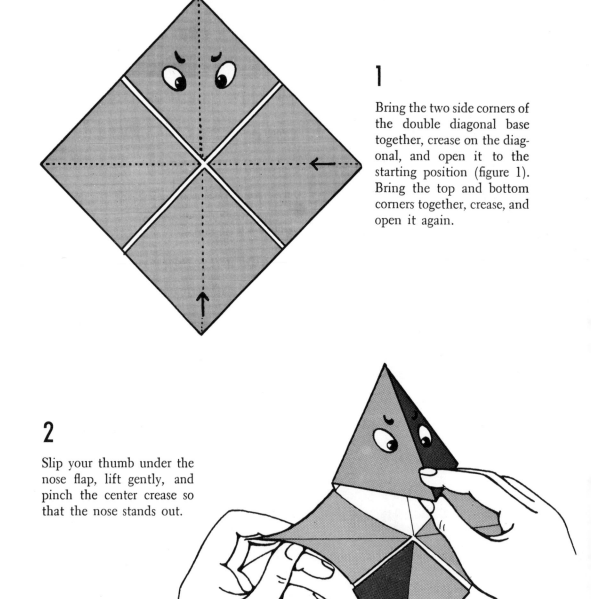

1

Bring the two side corners of the double diagonal base together, crease on the diagonal, and open it to the starting position (figure 1). Bring the top and bottom corners together, crease, and open it again.

2

Slip your thumb under the nose flap, lift gently, and pinch the center crease so that the nose stands out.

3

At each side corner, pinch the center fold closed. This will bring the upper and lower beaks together. Slip your pointer finger into the bird's mouth, press down on the crease in the center of the lower lip, and sharpen the crease with your thumb and middle finger. Now grasp firmly on each side of the mouth, and the slightest movement of your hands will make your Eating Bird eat.

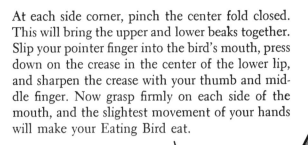

EATING BIRD

CHATTERBOX

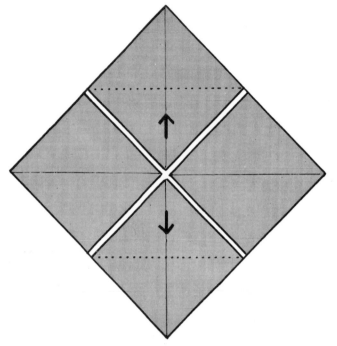

1

You will find four center flaps in the double diagonal base. Grasp the tip of the upper center flap and fold it so that the tip of the flap meets the top point of the double diagonal base. In the same way, fold the tip of the lower center flap to meet the bottom point of the base. These two triangles are the upper and lower halves of Chatterbox's face.

2

Bring the bottom point of the base up to meet the top point of the base. Crease sharply, and open it.

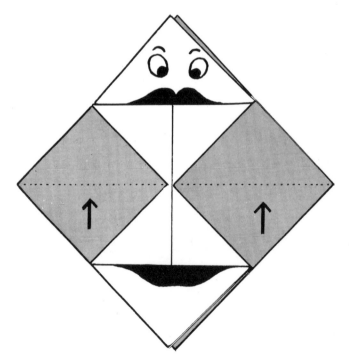

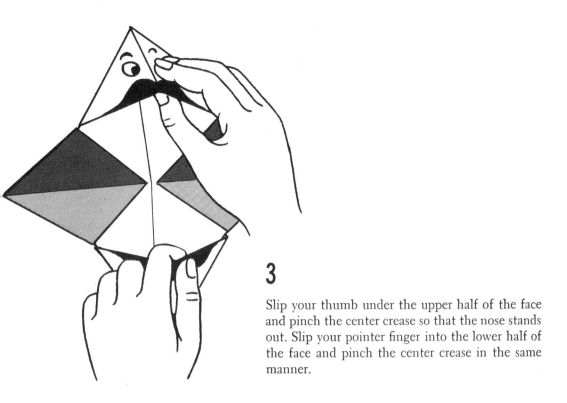

3

Slip your thumb under the upper half of the face and pinch the center crease so that the nose stands out. Slip your pointer finger into the lower half of the face and pinch the center crease in the same manner.

4

Place your thumb and pointer fingers under the double diagonal base at each side corner, pinching the center fold so that the two halves of the face are brought together. Move your fingers up to the sides of the mouth and by pushing your hands together and apart, you'll make Chatterbox chatter away.

A photograph of the finished puppet is on the next page ⬦

CHATTERBOX

CAT

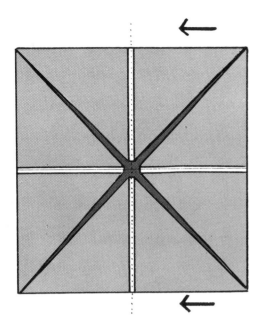

1

Turn the double diagonal base over. Bring the top edge down to meet the bottom edge, crease sharply, and open. Fold the right edge to meet the left edge. This time do not open.

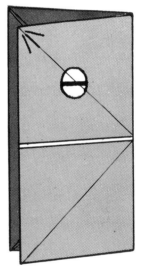

2

Lift the folded paper in your left hand. You will find four flaps along the right edge.

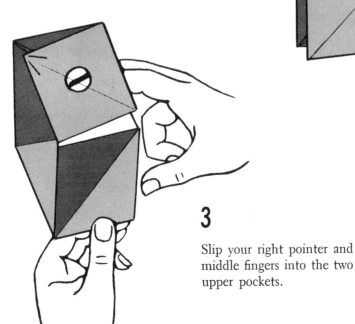

3

Slip your right pointer and middle fingers into the two upper pockets.

CAT Continued ◊

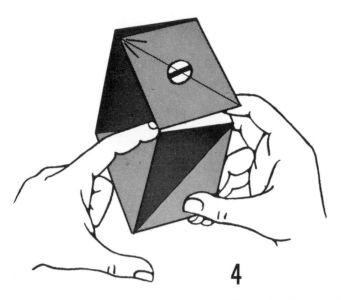

4

Grasp the lower right hand corner between your right thumb and ring finger. Insert your left pointer finger into the Cat's mouth.

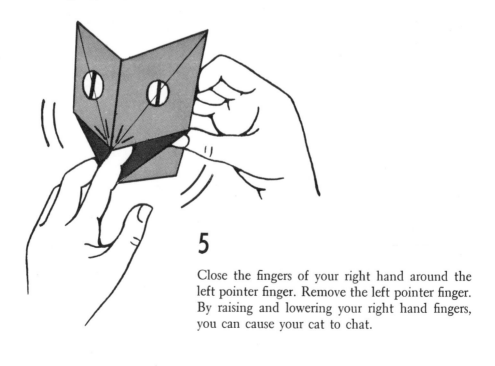

5

Close the fingers of your right hand around the left pointer finger. Remove the left pointer finger. By raising and lowering your right hand fingers, you can cause your cat to chat.

Original paper puppet created by Ligia Montoya

Oblong Base

Start the oblong base with *half* of a square.

1

Bring the lower edge of the rectangle to meet the upper edge. Crease sharply and open the paper.

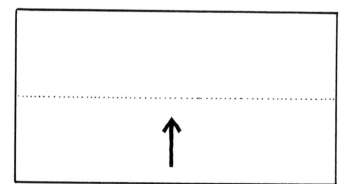

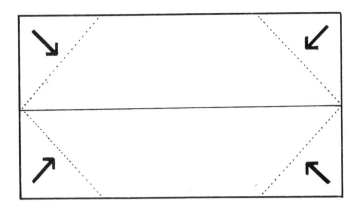

2

Fold each of the four corners to the center fold, so that your rectangle now comes to a sharp point at each side.

3

This is the oblong base.

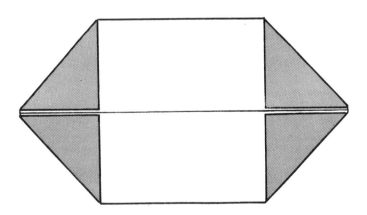

TALKING FISH

1

Fold the bottom edge of the oblong base to meet the top edge. Do *not* sharpen this fold.

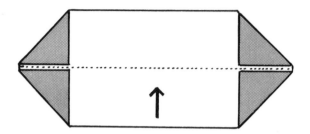

2

The center fold is now on the bottom.

3

With one hand at each corner, grasp the paper along the center fold. Roll your hands upward and toward one another, so that the center of the paper opens and the two points starts to meet.

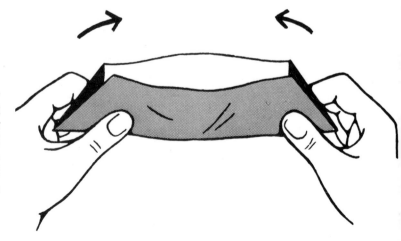

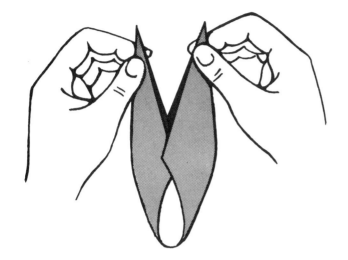

4

Slip the left point (and the two sides adjacent to the left point) into the right point.

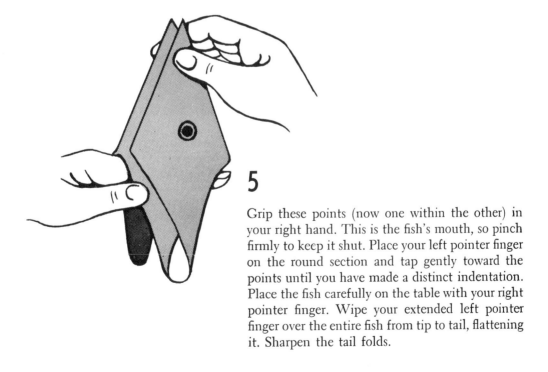

5

Grip these points (now one within the other) in your right hand. This is the fish's mouth, so pinch firmly to keep it shut. Place your left pointer finger on the round section and tap gently toward the points until you have made a distinct indentation. Place the fish carefully on the table with your right pointer finger. Wipe your extended left pointer finger over the entire fish from tip to tail, flattening it. Sharpen the tail folds.

TALKING FISH Continued ⟩

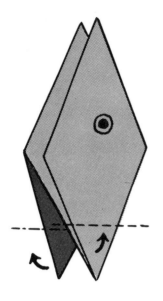

6

The tail is divided into two fins. Fold back the very tip of the upper fin. Turn the Fish over, and fold the other fin in the same way.

7

Grasp one of these tiny tail fins in each hand. When you pull your hands apart, the Fish's mouth will open.

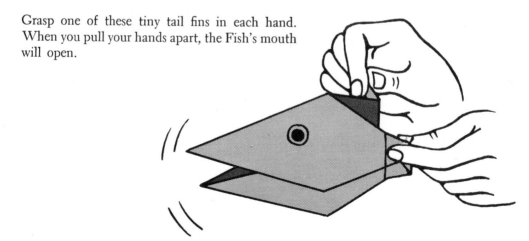

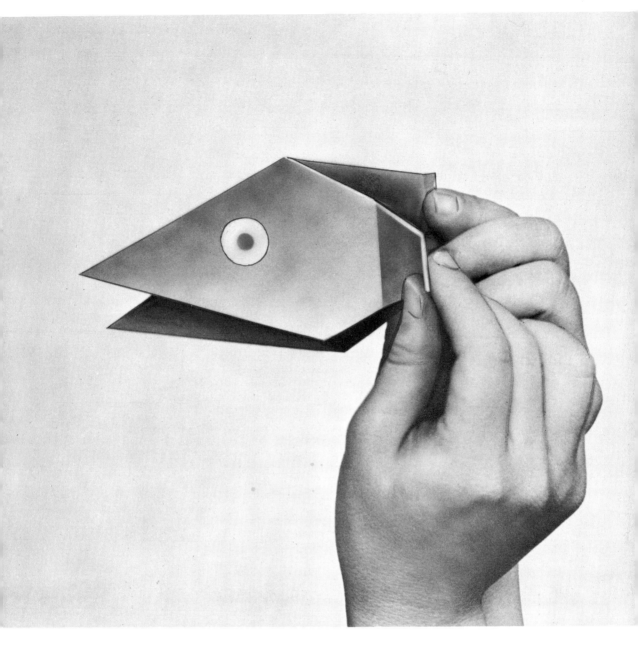

TALKING FISH

SNUB NOSE FISH

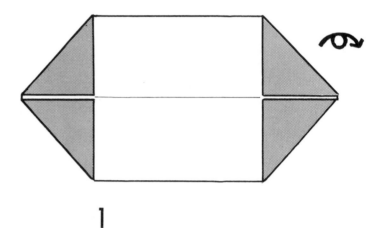

1

Turn the oblong base over.

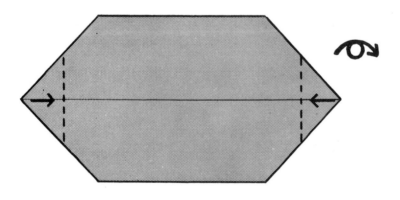

2

Fold the tip of the two side points to meet the center crease. Turn the paper over.

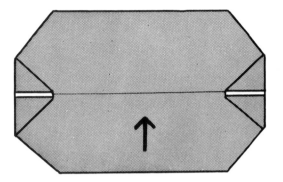

3

Fold the bottom edge up to meet the top edge. Now refer to figure #2 of the "Talking Fish" (page 42) and proceed as directed up to step #4. In Step #4, slip the left side into the right side until it touches the right center fold, but *do not force* the points to meet. Now proceed as directed through step #7. Your Snub Nose Fish will have a little turned up nose.

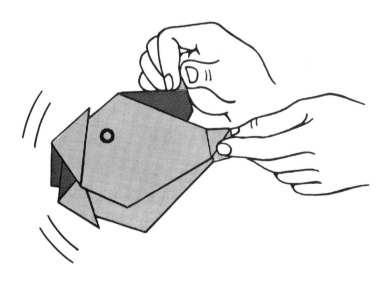

A photograph of the finished puppet is on the next page ▷

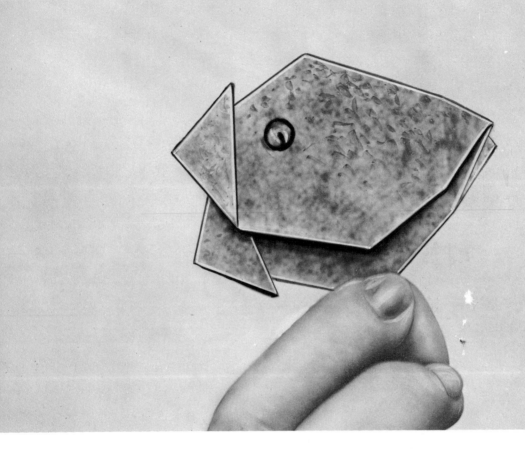

SNUB NOSE FISH

BIG MOUTH

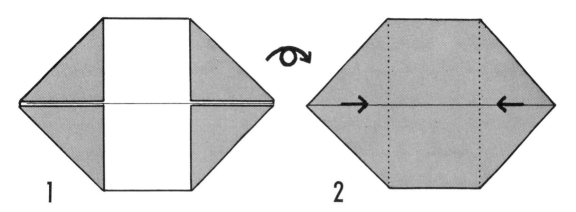

1

Make your oblong base with a piece of paper that is 8 inches by 12 inches or use a sheet from a large yellow "legal size" pad. Turn the oblong base over.

2

Fold in the two side points so that the paper is in thirds.

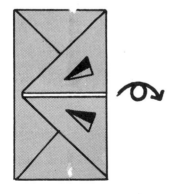

3

Turn the paper over and place it on the table in a horizontal position.

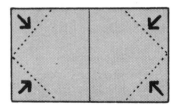

4

Fold in the side corners so that the rectangle comes to a sharp point on each side.

BIG MOUTH **Continued** ⟩

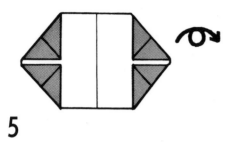

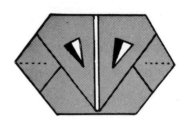

5

Turn the paper over.

6

Now the bottom lip is tucked under the top lip. There are two side corners. Place your pointer finger on top of a side corner, your thumb and middle finger below the paper, and pinch your pointer finger between your thumb and middle finger, pressing down to create a crease at the side corner. Do the same with the other side corner.

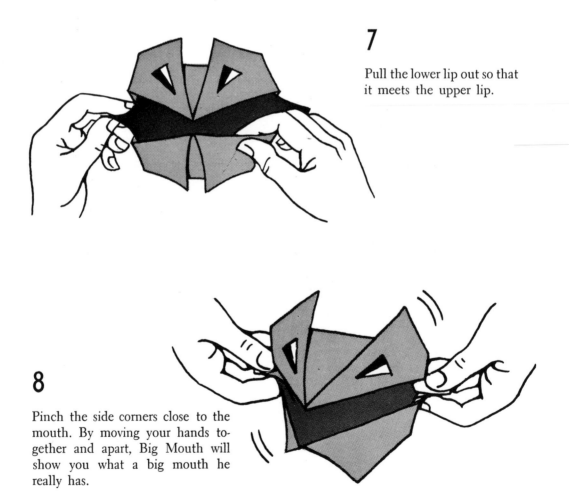

7

Pull the lower lip out so that it meets the upper lip.

8

Pinch the side corners close to the mouth. By moving your hands together and apart, Big Mouth will show you what a big mouth he really has.

Original paper puppet
created by
Lillian Oppenheimer

BIG MOUTH

SNAP DRAGON

1

Start with a square piece of paper and fold the top edge down to meet the bottom edge.

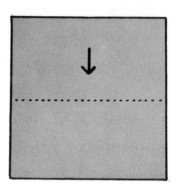

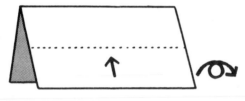

2

There are now two flaps, one in front and one in back. Fold the bottom edge of the front flap up to meet the center fold of the square. Turn the paper over.

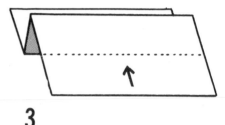

3

Bring the bottom of the flap facing you up to meet the center fold. Crease sharply and open this flap.

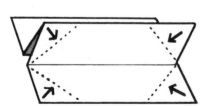

4

Fold the four corners facing you so that they meet this new center crease. Do *not* include the flap of paper in back.

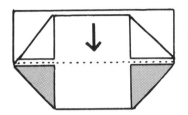

5

Fold the top edge down to meet the bottom edge. Once again, do *not* include the flap of paper in back.

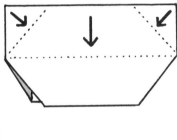

6

Now fold the two upper corners down to meet the center crease and bring the upper edge of this single flap down to meet the bottom edge of your model.

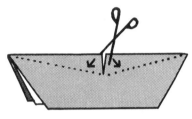

7

You now have two folded edges on top. At the middle of the center crease, cut or tear about a quarter of the way through both of these edges.

8

You have just created four separate lips. Fold both of the front lips down and turn the paper over.

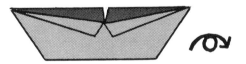

SNAP DRAGON Continued ▷

9

Fold both of the back lips down in the same way.

10

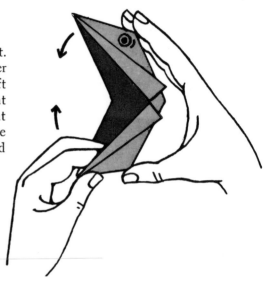

At the top of the model you have an open pocket. At the bottom, two points. Place your left pointer and middle fingers into the pocket with your left thumb resting on the bottom fold. Place your right thumb on one of the two points and your right pointer finger on the other point. Now bring these two fingers together. Remove your left hand and you will have closed the Snap Dragon's mouth.

11

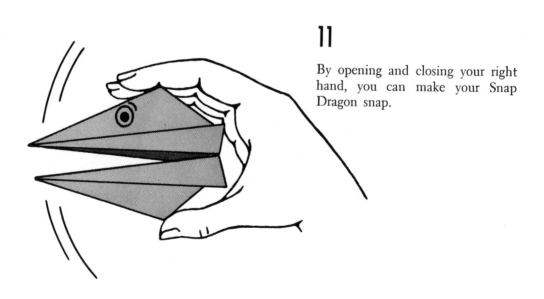

By opening and closing your right hand, you can make your Snap Dragon snap.

SNAP DRAGON

PIG

1

Start with a square piece of paper. Bring the two side points together. Then crease sharply and open the paper. Fold the top point down to meet the bottom point. Do not open.

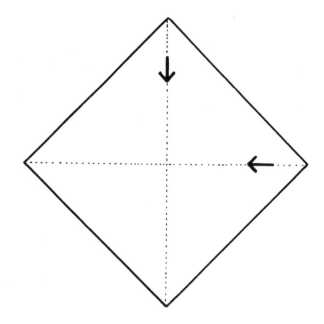

2

At the bottom point of the triangle there are two flaps. Fold the top flap up a bit. This creates the pig's snout.

3

Fold both of the side corners down to form ears. Let these ears cut across the sides of the face.

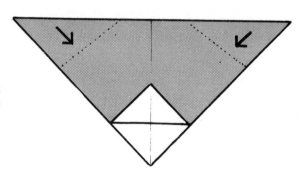

4

Fold the points of the ears up, allowing each point to extend just past the top edge of each ear.

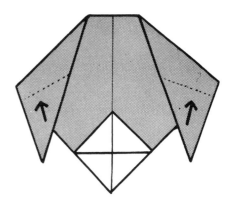

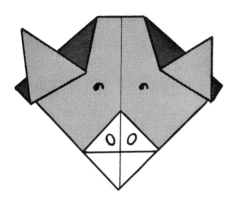

5

This is your Pig. He has a crease running down the front and back of his face. With your fingernail, carefully sharpen this crease in front and in back.

6

Grasp an ear in each hand, placing your fingers behind the upturned points of the ears. By moving your hands together and apart, you can make the Pig open and close his hungry little mouth.

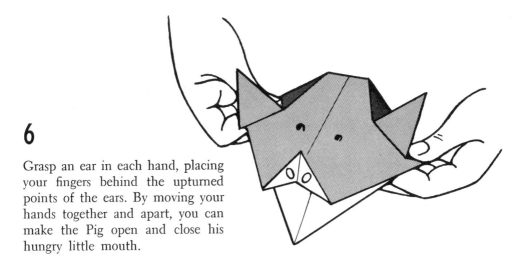

A photograph of the finished puppet is on the next page ▷

PIG

FOX

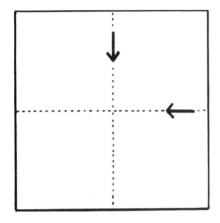

1

Bring the right edge of the square to meet the left edge. Crease sharply and open the paper. Then fold the top edge down to meet the bottom edge. Do *not* open.

2

Fold both sides to the center crease.

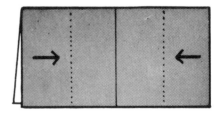

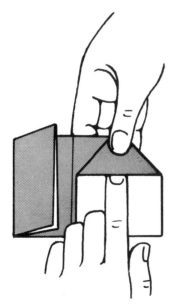

3

Lift the top layer of the right flap, insert your pointer finger and flatten the triangular "roof" that appears.

FOX *Continued* ▷

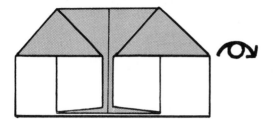

4

Repeat with the left flap, and turn the paper over.

5

Fold both sides to the center crease.

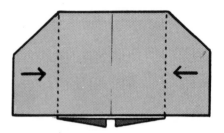

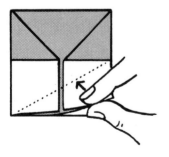

6

At the bottom of the paper, there are now two distinct layers. Lift only the upper layer and fold it diagonally from the lower left corner to the middle of the right side.

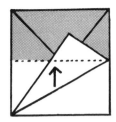

7

Now raise the lower left corner of the same layer as far as it will go and crease sharply.

8

Turn the paper over.

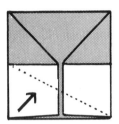

9

Repeat Step #6, folding diagonally from the lower right corner to the middle of the left side.

10

Raise the right corner as far as it will go.

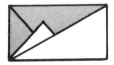

11

Crease sharply. The open "pocket" is now at the bottom.

FOX Continued ◊

12

Insert your right thumb and pointer finger into the corners of this "pocket."

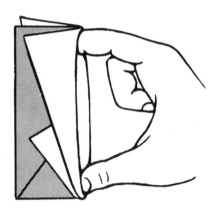

13

Press your left pointer finger against the center fold, and "bite" this finger with the fingers inside the pocket. Remove the left finger. By repeating this biting motion the Fox will talk — whether he's a sly fox or not is up to you!

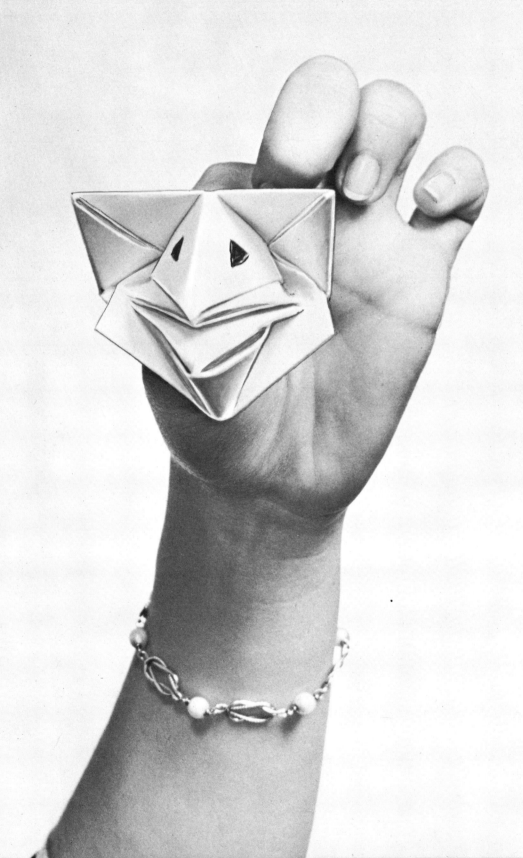

FLAPPING BIRD

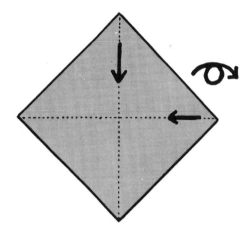

1

Bring the top point of the square down to meet the bottom point, crease sharply, and open the paper. Bring the two side points together, crease, and open. Turn the paper over.

2

Bring the side edges together, crease and open. Fold the top edge to meet the bottom edge. Do *not* open.

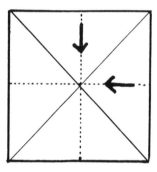

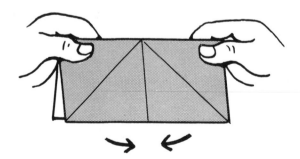

3

Grasping the upper corners, push your hands together. You now have four sections.

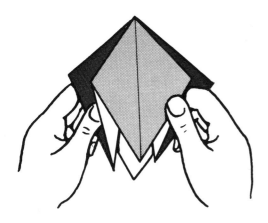

4

Flatten two of these sections on each side, forming a small square.

5

Lifting only the upper section on the right side, fold the open edge to meet the center crease. Repeat with the upper section on the left side.

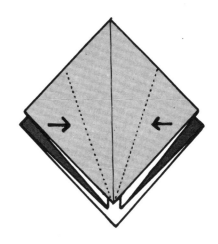

6

There is now a small angle on top. Bring down the point and crease along the base of this angle, and lift the point once again.

FLAPPING BIRD Continued ▷

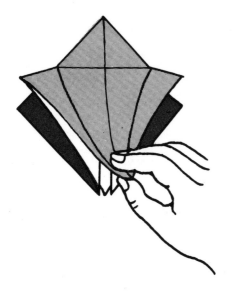

7

In step #5, you folded two sections to meet the center crease. Now run your pointer finger down this center crease, separating these two sections. At the very bottom point, lift the point of the single top layer.

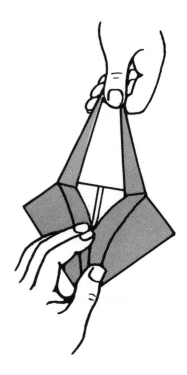

8

Pinch together the layer exposed by lifting the point, simultaneously pulling this point as far as it can go, until you have formed a long diamond. Flatten and crease the edges.

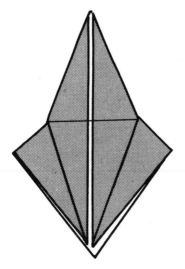

9

Turn the paper over and repeat steps #5, 6, 7, 8.

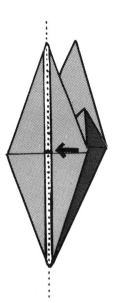

10

On the right side, there are two layers, one on top of the other. Life only the top layer, and fold this right side point to meet the left side point.

11

Turn the paper over. You now have three layers on the right side. Once again, lift only the top layer and fold the right side point to meet the left side point.

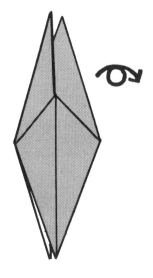

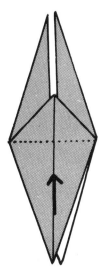

12

At the bottom of your diamond, you have two wings. Lift the wing facing you and fold it up so that the tip of the wing meets the two points at the top of the diamond. Turn the paper over and fold up the other wing, so that the four points meet on top.

FLAPPING BIRD Continued ◊

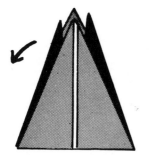

13

Hold the triangle in your right hand. On top, there are two inner points between the two wings.

14

Grasp the left inner point between your pointer and middle fingers and pull this point out to form the bird's neck. With your thumb and ring fingers, pinch the folds at the base of the neck to keep the neck in this position.

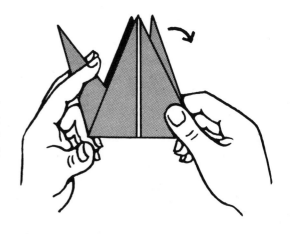

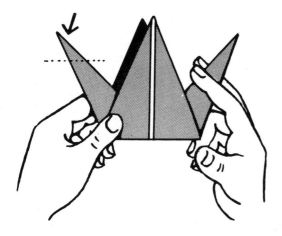

15

In the same way, pull out the right inner point. To form the bird's head, fold the tip of the neck down at an angle, crease sharply, and then fold back and forth along this same crease. Now straighten the point. (You've created a slanting crease.)

16

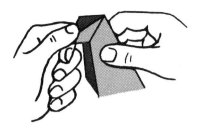

With your right hand, pinch the center fold of the neck directly below this slanting crease. Place your left pointer finger into the pocket under the center crease, so that it opens the center crease at the top point only. Put your left thumb on top of the center crease, pinching the point between these two fingers, and pull down until the center crease reverses itself and forms a valley between your two hands. With your left hand, sharpen all these new creases.

17

Now with your left hand, grasp the middle of the bird. Gently roll the wing around your right pointer finger. Curl the other wing in the same way.

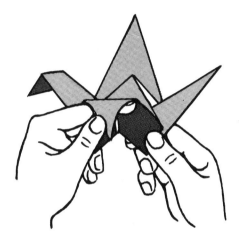

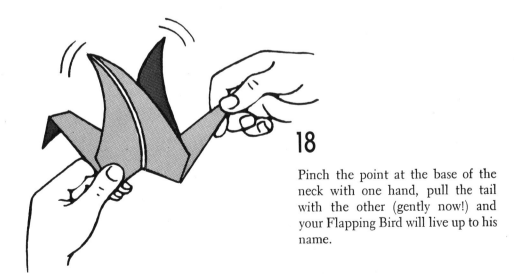

18

Pinch the point at the base of the neck with one hand, pull the tail with the other (gently now!) and your Flapping Bird will live up to his name.

A photograph of the finished puppet is on the next page ▷

SIMPLE SUE

1

Simple Sue can be drawn on the back of a calling card or on any small paper rectangle.

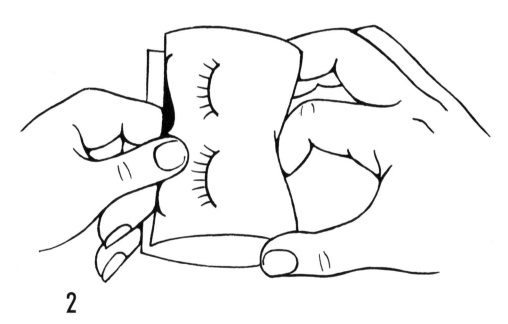

2

Bend, but do not fold, the rectangle in half with your left thumb on top, middle finger on the bottom, and your pointer finger sandwiched between the two layers. Place your right thumb and middle finger on opposite sides at the bend of the paper. Press the knuckle of your right pointer finger against this bend until you create a slight indentation.

SIMPLE SUE Continued ◊

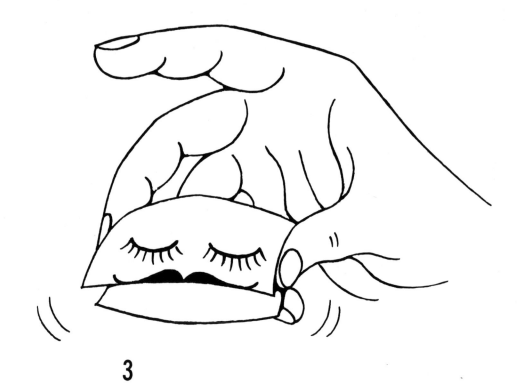

3

Now, lift this right pointer finger, and take away your left hand. Simply press your right thumb and middle finger together slightly and Simple Sue will speak for herself.

Original paper puppet created
by George Sands

SIMPLE SUE

ON TEACHING ORIGAMI

There is no doubt that Mrs. Lillian Oppenheimer is the most experienced teacher of paperfolding in the United States. Her method is to weave into the instructions points of interest or information so that the student — child or adult — will be entertained as well as instructed. What follows is a transcript of a lesson as given by Mrs. Oppenheimer which demonstrates her teaching technique. Obviously, the teacher will want to use other stories or information that might interest the particular student, and what follows should therefore be considered mainly as general guidelines to a technique that has worked well.

"Try to imagine the Japan or China of a hundred years ago — no radio or television, no telephone or electric light or movies, no automobile or trains or planes — hundreds upon thousands of families too poor to buy toys for their children — but having paper, which was, by the way, a Chinese invention. At the end of a day's work, the family would gather together for the evening meal and the grandparents or parents, in order to amuse the children, would teach them how to paperfold. From a Chinese friend, I learned that as a child Origami was one of her few sources for amusement and recreation. She had never owned a store bought toy, but through Origami she was taught how to fold dolls and doll clothes and in this way she made her own playthings. Above all else she was happiest when she could show her mother a new folded figure she had created.

"The paperfold animal we are now going to make together is not new. In fact it is one of the oldest and most intriguing examples of Origami. The Japanese have been teaching the Flapping Bird for hundreds of years and each new generation is charmed by its graceful movements. See if you don't feel the same way about it.

"First place your square of paper before you like a diamond and crease it in half by bringing the lower point to the upper point. I used to call this a 'diaper fold' until the younger generation pointed out to me that diapers are not folded the way I used to do it forty years ago when I was raising a family. Now open the paper and rotate it clockwise to bring the crease you have just made straight up and down in front of you. Again lift the lower point to the upper point, crease firmly, and open the paper. Since people all over the world have fun with paperfolding, we try to use an international terminology whenever possible. Every country has mountains and valleys. If you look at the paper you have just creased twice, you will find that you have made a cross of what paperfolders call 'valley folds.' Turn the paper over and you will notice that a cross of two 'mountain folds' is facing you.

"Fold this paper like a book, bring the lower edge of the square to the upper edge. Crease sharply and open the paper. Now make a second book fold by rotating the paper and creasing it in the same way as before. It is interesting to note that a German, Friedrich Froebel, was the first person to use the terminology of 'book fold', 'cupboard fold', etc. He was also the man who gave us the word 'kindergarten.'

"Open the paper at this point and check to see if your work is correct. You should see alternating mountain and valley folds. Most of the creasing in Origami is making preparation folds. If these folds have been done properly, the paper will do your bidding at the slightest touch. Right here is a case in point. You have prepared your square with alternating mountain and valley folds. Bring the lower edge of the paper to the upper edge in the valley book fold you have just made and, pinching the lower folded edges firmly, push your hands together and the four corners will now meet making a shape that resembles an umbrella. You now have four double corners, with two on the right and two on the left. Sharpen all the creases firmly.

"Place your model in front of you with the closed apex away from you and the open or free points toward you. Again you should have two double corners to the right and two to the left. We will work with the two upper layers first. Take the top double corner on the right and fold it to the center laying the raw edge on the center crease. Repeat this action with the top double corner on the left and you have now made what I call an 'ice cream cone' fold. Once when I was instructing some children we came to this point and one of my pupils cried out 'What do we do with the ice cream, Mrs. Oppenheimer?' After questioning him, I found out that he was referring to the triangle above the cone. Fold this 'ice cream' triangle forward and backward as far as it will go, making a 'mountain fold' and a 'valley fold' on the same crease.

"Now we are ready to lift up the wings of this lovely bird. The model in front of you should look like a double ice cream cone. Slightly opening the right and left sections of the 'cone' run your finger down between them as though they were the doors of a cupboard and find the hidden point at the bottom of the cone. Lift this point up high and see the duplicate 'ice cream cone' creases in the layer of paper that has just been exposed. With one hand, pinch these creases together and with the other hand continue to lift the point and lay it back on itself until you have formed a long diamond with the two raw edges having come together in the center. Crease all the folds. Turn the model over and repeat this with the other 'ice cream cone'. Believe it or not, you have made the bird's wings.

"Now hold your model so that the wings are pointing up and the lower part is divided. It is time to perform a kind of paperfolding miracle. There are two points to the right of the center of your model and two to the left. Fold the upper right layer over to the upper left layer as if you were turning the pages in a book. Now there are three points to the left and only one to the right. Turn the whole model over so that there are three points on the right and once more fold the upper right hand point over to the left hand point. The minor miracle has been accomplished. Wasn't it easy? Once I was teaching a group and at this point a man cried out, 'It may be a minor miracle to you, Mrs. Oppenheimer, but for me, it's a major catastrophe.' I hope it wasn't for you.

"Now the divided part is on the top and the wing is pointing down. Lift up the one in the front and fold it over; lift the one in the back and fold it over. There are now four points on the top. To make the bird's neck, pull the inner point on the left downward until it forms a right angle to the triangle and crease it firmly. Do the same thing with the inner point on the right to make the bird's tail. To make the bird's head, grasp the point at the top of the neck and fold it down between the sides of the neck, and crease.

"Now curl the wings away from the rear of the bird by pulling them gently through your fingers. Hold the bird firmly by the point of the breast and grasping on the tail, pull it back and forth and the bird will flap its wings."

Wherever I have taught Origami, in schools, hospitals, to church groups, scouts, or just one child, paperfolding has been greeted with great enthusiasm, for it is a joy to take a simple piece of paper and fold it and crease it into so many recognizable and beautiful shapes. The expression of delight that dimples the face of a new folder when he completes his first model is more than enough compensation for the intrigued teacher.

by LILLIAN OPPENHEIMER

BIBLIOGRAPHY

There are many books on Origami available in libraries and bookstores. The following list is not intended to be a complete paperfolding bibliography, but rather a selection of works each of which has particular values.

THE ART OF CHINESE PAPERFOLDING, Maying Soong, Harcourt, Brace and World, 1948, New York $2.95. Mrs. Soong describes about thirty models. Particularly charming are the lighthouse and pagoda bookmarks and the furniture. Even beginners in paperfolding will have very little difficulty with Mrs. Soong's clearly illustrated figures.

THE ART OF ORIGAMI, Samuel Randlett, E. P. Dutton & Co., 1961, New York $5.95. Among the many figures in this book, the author has included forty of his original models. It is clearly illustrated with drawings by his wife and includes a scholarly treatise concerning various bases and basic folds, an extensive bibliography, a chapter on teaching methods, and information on sources of paper. There is also an erudite introduction by Edward Kallop, Associate Curator of Exhibitions at Cooper Union Museum for the Arts of Decoration. Mr. Randlett's analytical approach to Origami is to be commended.

EL MUNDO DE PAPEL, Dr. Nemesio Montero, Editorian Sever-Cuesta, 1939, Valladolid, Spain, $2.00. THE WORLD OF PAPER offers eighty-five models and ignorance of Spanish need not be a barrier. The illustrations are clear and the book contains a wealth of valuable material.

KAYARAGUSE (Vol. 8), Katsuyuki Adachi, Pine Cone Press, 1961, Washington D.C. $10.00. Mr. and Mrs. Martin Brossman devoted years to searching for this lost Origami encyclopedia. They were finally successful and have published a most faithful reproduction of the hand-drawn portion containing over thirty models. A "must" for the serious student of Origami and a "find" for the collector.

ORIGAMI ZUKAN, Okimasa Uchiyama, Hirkari no Kuni, 1958, Tokyo, $2.75. The purist will find in this Japanese book that too much cutting is necessary (Origami is the art of folding paper into figures *without* cutting) but the beautiful flowers, furniture and human figures will be compensation enough. This book is used in schools in Japan and is the only one recommended by the Master, Akira Yoshizawa.

PAPERFOLDING FOR BEGINNERS, William D. Murray and Francis J. Rigney, Dover Press, 1960, New York, $1.00. This valuable little paper-back book contains over forty figures. It finishes with a paperfolding story, "How Charlie Bought His Boat," illustrated with a single sheet of paper which is folded and re-folded making one object after another as the story proceeds.

PAPER MAGIC, Robert Harbin, Oldbourne Press, 1956, London, $3.75. An excellent portrayal of more than a hundred models, this book also contains some very interesting historical facts about paperfolding.

POCKET GUIDE TO ORIGAMI, Isao Honda, Asahi Origami Club, 1959, Tokyo, $1.00. This paperback book describes sixteen figures. Models of three complete figures are attached and a packet of Origami paper is included.

All of these books as well as special Origami paper are available through the American Origami Center, 71 West 11-Street, New York 11, New York.

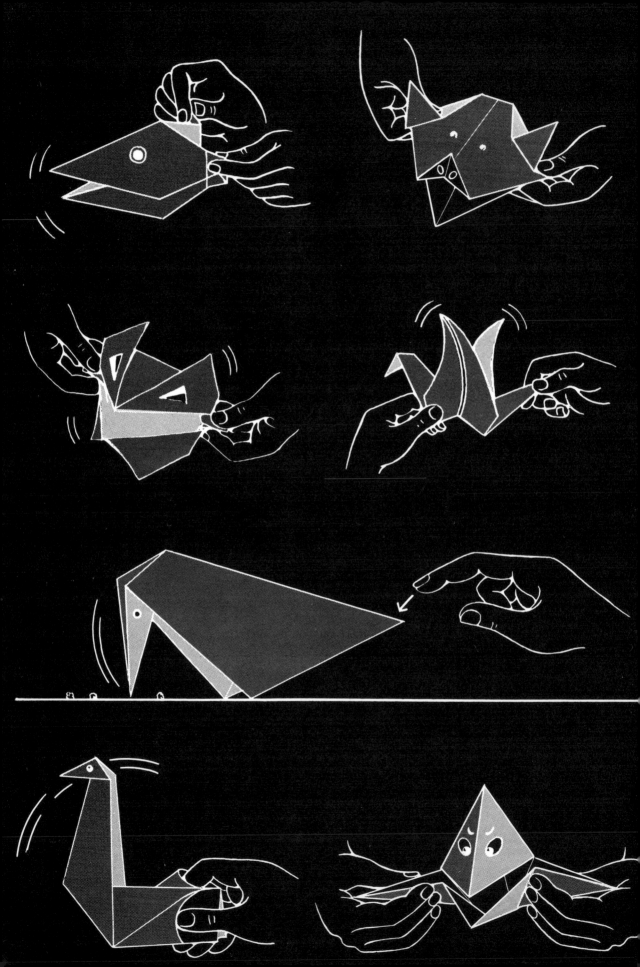